WRITERS

ON

WRITERS

Published in partnership with

STATE LIBRARY
VICTORIA
What's your story?

WRITERS
ERIK JENSEN
ON
KATE JENNINGS
WRITERS

Black Inc.

Published by Black Inc.
in association with the University of Melbourne and State Library Victoria.

Black Inc., an imprint of Schwartz Publishing Pty Ltd
Level 1, 221 Drummond Street, Carlton VIC 3053, Australia
enquiries@blackincbooks.com • www.blackincbooks.com

State Library Victoria
328 Swanston Street, Melbourne VIC 3000, Australia
www.slv.vic.gov.au

The University of Melbourne
Parkville VIC 3010, Australia
www.unimelb.edu.au

National Library of Australia Cataloguing-in-Publication entry:
Jensen, Erik, author.
On Kate Jennings / Erik Jensen.
9781863959834 (hardback)
9781925435818 (ebook)
Jennings, Kate, 1948–
Women authors, Australian – Biography.
Expatriate authors – United States – Biography.
Authors, Australian – United States – Biography.

Extract from 'Home Suite' in *Selected Poems* © 2007 by Les Murray.
Reprinted with permission of Les Murray and Margaret Connolly.

Cover and text design by Peter Long
Photograph of Erik Jensen: Siân Scott-Clash
Photograph of Kate Jennings: Wayne Taylor/Fairfax Media

Printed in China by 1010 International.

For Nell

'Life is short … the occasion fleeting;
experience deceitful, and judgment difficult.'
Hippocrates

Kate and I met for the first time in the cold of a New York winter, her brain hot with zoster virus. A sickness was scratching inside her skull, pushing on the backs of her eye sockets.

She blinked at me as we stood outside the restaurant. There was a pause, made long by the weather. 'You look threadbare,' she said, finally. 'All Australians are threadbare.'

This was half a dozen years ago. Later, I told the poet Jennifer Clement about the exchange. She said: 'You must steal that straight into a novel.'

I had looked up Kate because I was a fan of her essays – pieces about her life, mostly, ruthless in their precision. At lunch, she talked about everything. She talked without prompt or hesitation. When the bill came, she looked at me again. 'I'm sorry if I said anything awful. It's this damned zoster. It does things.'

* * *

She calls her Girlie and him Boy.

She calls their mother Irene and their father Rex.

She calls their town Progress. The bush is full of savage irony.

She says their father is a good man, but disappointed. He grew up on chalk soil, a blighted soil. His family tilled it for wheat. He stayed home from school one harvest and never went back.

She says their mother is cold and sarcastic. She has expectations. Irene passes a harshness on to her children. They grow up ignoring their father.

They are hers and not his.

Kate does not wait. She says most of this on the very first page.

*   *   *

She was writing a poem but it wasn't working.

She read *Annie John* by Jamaica Kincaid. She felt for the sense of character, the smallness of the story, the uncomplicated curiosity of children. Kincaid's novel begins with a superstition made from childhood. It reads: 'For a short while during the year I was ten, I thought only people I did not know died.'

Kate realised she was writing a book.

*   *   *

Irene's wedding ends in her parents' garden. A climbing lily is in bloom. Kate uses its Latin name – *Gloriosa superba* – to hide the cruelty of the image.

Irene's family is Anglican and rich. They are so certain, so complacent, they resemble well-stuffed sofas. Friends think of Irene as fast. Her parents sleep in separate bedrooms.

Rex, a bridesmaid notices, is bewildered, like a schoolboy who has lost his lunch money. A sister thinks he is as interesting as a month of wet Sundays. He has returned from the Victory March in London, but in retelling it can only think to mention the neck of the man marching in front of him. His parents are well scrubbed and talcumed, out of place in this house. The neck, in his story, is dirty. He recalls this with a bleat of nervous laughter. Earlier, he thought about crying.

The house at which Rex and Irene arrive is raised on wood posts. Pigface is in bloom. Kate does not dress up its name. A step on the verandah is loose and Rex promises to fix it. 'His tone annoyed Irene,' Kate writes. 'She brushed the feeling away, but it re-formed, hovered, settled, like a mantle of flies on a hot day.'

Later, it 'grew in her like an iris rhizome, bulbous and knotted, to be divided and planted elsewhere, time and again'.

*　*　*

Kate Jennings was born Catherine and spent her first years as Cathy. To family, she still is Cathy.

She was born in Temora and grew up in Hanwood, in the New South Wales Riverina. On one side was the town of Yoogali. On the other, Willbriggie. There was a primary school, a convent and a post office. The year was 1948. The population was just on fifty.

'I remember far too much,' Kate says. 'I always say I have got a terrible memory, but I dredge it up. I was so very lonely. And at the mercy of my mother.' Later, she says: 'While I remember a lot, when I was living it I didn't comprehend much. I didn't understand sex, not in the least, and that would seem to have been bubbling away under the surface all the time. Ineluctable. I wanted out, to go to Sydney, and be a poet.'

Kate has a younger brother. His name is Dare.

*   *   *

Irene has Girlie in one chapter and Boy in a chapter one after that. It is page 36.

As she lies in hospital, Girlie purpled-faced and breastfeeding, Irene can think only of a cat she saw in the woodheap, eating the kitten it had just birthed. The creature was still trapped in its caul.

Girlie's mouth strays from the nipple and she butts her screwed-up face against Irene's chest. A midwife comes to help and Irene curses her. Later, Irene has the baby with her on a bicycle when she bumps over a rut in the road and the little girl's foot is caught in the spokes. Irene feels only irritation.

*   *   *

The book is called *Snake*. I read it on the flight to LA, under a circle of yellow light and the blinking of the seatbelt sign. The images crackled in my head as I waited for the connecting flight to New York: the pigs as they ate Irene's flowers; the cave of a bathroom in which she had Boy read to her; the sheep carcass alive with maggots.

The edition was a late one, published by Black Inc. The text on the back called it 'a modern classic'. On the front Shirley Hazzard called it 'irresistibly good'. When I met Kate the next morning, I said nothing about it.

*   *   *

The poem Kate was writing was called 'Deserta Rerum'.

'I have a clear memory,' she says, 'of trying to write descriptions of life on that barren Quandary hill. Snagged on what mulesing is like in the shade of the bonny ironbark trees. Or maybe it was the castration and tailing of lambs. Flick of a knife. Never came back to the subject, I think. I do remember thinking I could do better with prose.'

The poem became one of two anchors in her second collection. It lacked the immediacy of her other work, however. It was written at a distance, with an academic text for reference.

Throughout, she quoted from a 1966 comparative study of irrigation: *Water and Land* by Trevor Langford-Smith and John Rutherford. These men were not poets.

She also quoted Eleanor Clarke: 'It is important to see well and remember distinctly ... otherwise you wallow in sentiment, and that is disgusting.'

And from Ray Mathew's final play:

> Peter: It's not a bad view.
> Kerry: I was born here; it's not a view.

In its last four stanzas, the poem shifted forward out of childhood, to the glimpses she would get as she looked back. The change in register made for an intimate correspondence. It ended the way her father's letters did: 'Love, as ever, Dad.'

*　*　*

When Kate was two she had rheumatic fever. She was in hospital for six weeks. Her first memory is of her legs aching. Her mother was forbidden to pick her up. Her next memory is of starting school at the age of five. After that, she says, she remembers everything. She says it is a curse.

'Here's something I remembered,' she says, unprompted. 'I was walking down the road to go to school. I can remember the hat I had on. And I fell backwards and gashed the whole top of my head open, which had to be shaved off and stitched up. At the same time I had boils. I had boils all over. I had boils in my ears and on my bottom. These are the sorts of things you got in those ages. I used to have to go to school with a beanie and a cushion.'

* * *

Rerum, Kate instructed, was from a seventeenth-century term for a fascicle of loosely arranged notes.

The earth in the poem was red and furrowed. Her father's pant leg was stuck with paspalum. The channels were saucers of brackish back-up water.

Her mother had dreams that had begun to fester. She chose her husband because he could dance. Her mode was Irene's: 'The more aggrieved she became, the more vivid her garden.'

Snake was waiting in other poems, too. It lay dead still in the final line of one titled 'Sports Day, 1955': 'We called him Boy until he wasn't.'

*   *   *

Kate's mother was one of six children. Kate doesn't say her name. She calls her 'Mum'. She calls her mother's family 'the other side'. They were rich, a family of lawyers and politicians. Her grandfather made his money drying fruit. He learnt the technique in California.

Kate's father's name was Laurence. He was tall and good at dancing. Hail ruined his parents' first wheat crop and they lived the rest of their lives in the shadow of that failure. Kate calls them 'hardscrabble farmers'. Laurence left school at the age of twelve and never went back.

Kate's mother was engaged to an American soldier but it did not take. The romance produced a ring and nothing more. Kate's father served in the Middle East and then New Guinea. Few in his regiment survived. Once, his tent was strafed while he was out for a smoke. 'He said, "You know, I had a lucky war. And then I met your mother."'

Kate's parents lived at Quandary and it was.

*   *   *

Snake is a poet's novel, built of accruing stanzas. The whole book is shot through with angry truth.

Kate picks out her chapters with unmarked quotations. The two best are: 'You Know Bert I Sometimes Marvel Women Can Go Sour Like That' and 'Dawn Comes Slowly and Changes Nothing'. The truest is: 'Home Is the First and Final Poem'.

The sour one is Henry Green. The dawn is Philip Levine. The last is Les Murray:

Home is the first
and final poem
and every poem between
has this mum home seam.

*   *   *

The first snake isn't there. Irene watches for it all the same, as she picks through paspalum clumps to gather asparagus. She plans to eat this with white sauce and corned beef.

Specifically, it is a brown snake that worries Irene. She looks for the dull glittering of scales. The narrator warns that they are long, fast and deadly.

'The snake thing has all kinds of meanings,' Kate says. 'I remember looking it up: it also has all kinds of sexual connotations. You guys have to live with these damn things.'

*   *   *

Decent is the word Kate uses to describe her father. She says he dressed well and was proud. He loved dogs.

She recalls being ten or twelve and coming home from school. She and her father were talking about something that happened in town. It was a rare conversation. He seldom spoke. 'I remember him turning to me once and saying, "Everybody needs somebody to hate,"' she says. 'He was right about that. He passed that little piece of wisdom on. He didn't talk much, but he did tell me that … A blunt fact.'

Earlier, she recalls her mother, a high-school state swimmer, dressing her in water wings and throwing her into the deep end of the Griffith Olympic Pool. The only instruction she gave Kate was a single word: 'Swim.'

In an essay, decades later, Kate wrote: 'A big believer in deep ends, my mother.'

*   *   *

Snake is the great Australian novel. That is what I start telling people. I give as gifts three dozen copies. I see the book at a house I've never visited and open it to find my own inscription: 'As promised, the Great Australian Novel.'

I send a copy to Ian Donaldson, the renowned Jonson scholar, former professor of English at Cambridge and a fellow of King's College. He reads it in a single restless night. 'The great Australian novel?' he writes the next morning. 'Yes, I'd agree, it certainly warrants that sort of ranking, though that phrase as conventionally used conjures up a kind of laborious realism which *Snake* so spectacularly lacks. I loved its spareness, its brevity, its ability – like the creature it mimics – to strike without warning then vanish without trace.'

This essay is a love letter. It is also a thankyou note.

*   *   *

Kate was fourteen when she realised she was a writer. 'It was school compositions – and I think it's in the book. I started writing these great long stories for my compositions, by hand. They were great big adventure compositions where a girl did very well for herself, going around the world, having adventures. And I would make people sit down and listen to me. That's probably where it started, I think.'

The same year, Kate sat at her mother's typewriter and produced her first poetry manuscript. She kept a copy. It is terrible.

'A whole pile of people I knew were going to be writers,' she says. 'They were all going to write the great Australian novel. And they didn't.'

*   *   *

The next snake is a line from *Antony and Cleopatra*. It is a crown, an invention of betrayal, a fury at a messenger. The next snake is Irene, silent with resentment.

The snake after that belongs to D.H. Lawrence. It is the heading of Chapter 10, Part II: 'In Sicily the Black, Black Snakes Are Innocent, the Gold Are Venomous'.

In his poem, Lawrence waits at a water-trough to fill his pitcher. There is a snake ahead of him, drinking. In its presence he feels honoured and afraid. His is a folly of emotion, of perversity and cowardice, and when he finally tries to strike the snake and fails he feels pettiness and remorse.

The next line in the poem, after the one Kate borrowed, is:

And voices in me said, If you were a man

You would take a stick and break him now, and finish him off.

* * *

The compositions Kate mentioned start on page 64. Girlie wins a prize for one on page 72.

'Girlie was the opposite of Boy: eager, earnest, graceless. She threw herself into everything, whether she was good at it or not, whether she enjoyed it or not,' Kate writes.

'Nobody liked her. Children thought she was a know-it-all, adults recoiled from her neediness. She cornered anyone she could and read them her compositions, which were of epic proportions and always featured a girl like herself – a *fearless* girl – having improbable adventures: captaining a submarine in the Arctic Circle or a junk in the China Seas. Girlie numbered her books and kept everyone up to date on the current figure.'

The prize Girlie wins is for an essay on Simpson and his donkey. She reads it on the radio as part of an Anzac Day broadcast. The essay is streaked with blood and broken bodies. Simpson labours between bursting shells, doughty despite his work.

Kate does not leave Girlie's success unpunished. She writes: 'She used words like "intrepid," "tenacious," and "selfless," and imagined herself to have some of these virtues.'

* * *

Kate worked for two winters on Long Island, the sky pulled over her like a heavy blanket. She said the sea there was angry. She rode a bicycle and looked after a friend's dogs.

'It's much easier to write about something – and people – when you're not anywhere near them,' she says. 'You don't care what they think about you. You just do it.'

She laughs. 'You have to move if you're going to write about anyone, I think. I mean, it's freeing. And then when anybody gets upset or carries on, you've forgotten about that bit.'

* * *

Rex is quiet. He works and does not talk. Sometimes he is pinned to the wall by his wife's moods. In an expressive moment he allows himself to take off his shoes and wade into an irrigation channel, enjoying the mud between his toes.

Mostly, though, his character is muted. 'He was muted,' Kate says. 'When he was married to Mum, he hardly spoke. We ate quickly and got away. We didn't talk at the dinner table.'

* * *

At school, she was good. She was wide-eyed when she realised later that others were not. 'The closest I came to experimenting with adulthood was several furtive cigarettes and a bumbling kiss that left me witless down by the pigsty between dances at Yanco Agricultural School.'

Kate keeps a Cibachrome picture of herself at the age of ten, standing in front of a bed of pigface and alyssum. She is wearing a dress her mother made, decorated with white ribbon. Behind her is a stand of roses a little taller than she is. Everything is in bloom. The lawn is couch.

*　　*　　*

Six pages after Boy is born, Irene is unfaithful for the first time. She writes a letter for the American soldier to whom she had been engaged. She says she wishes the child were his. She has given it his name. She puts the letter in an unsealed envelope and waits for Rex to find it.

Kate writes that Rex reads it 'in an agony of disbelief'. He is not surprised. So changed is he by it that he cannot remember a time when he was innocent of its contents. He thinks about leaving.

Two pages later Irene is at Yoogali. Kate doesn't change the town's name. There is a dance at the Catholic Club. While Rex is inside, Irene lets a friend of his push her against a car beside the church hall. Her skirt is rucked up and her underpants pulled down. Kate writes that she revels in the obliteration and the deceit. 'Years later,' Kate judges, 'she would remember the feel of the cold metal against her bare backside.'

* * *

There was no television but Kate read *Mad* magazine and copies of *Time* her mother got in. Dare listened to *The Goon Show* as if it were the sacrament. Their mother read to them Banjo Paterson and *The Song of Hiawatha* and Kate caught the rhythm of it. They were Church of England and she read *The Book of Common Prayer*. With city cousins, they travelled every summer to Narrabeen on the northern beaches. 'I did know there was a huge wide world out there.'

Kate's father went to Sydney and brought back a rifle for Dare and a *Pears' Cyclopedia* for Kate. The boys at school got hold of it and made fun of the diagrams of naked women and bodily functions inside. Kate was desperately embarrassed. 'I was clearly very different from the other kids but I was a part of them. It's hard not to be in small towns.'

* * *

Rex wonders if there isn't something wrong with Irene. He thinks of a woman who drowned her toddlers in a dam. He lets his arms hang by his sides and asks her to have a heart.

Rex doesn't talk about the war. When his children ask about the ivory chopsticks in the desk in the living room, he tells them to go outside and play.

When an army mate visits, they drink a demijohn of sherry. It is the only time Girlie has seen her father drunk. Irene waits in the kitchen, drinking cold tea. The two men take turns pissing on her crepe myrtle.

* * *

Kate says she was mostly miserable, except for when she was swimming, playing hockey or reading. She says her childhood was never simple, never uncomplicated. 'Because of Mum. You can't live with a woman like that. She was having affairs left, right and centre. All kinds of silly buggers was going on. I was probably aware of it on a very little level. Dare might have been more aware of it.'

She says her mother taught her nothing about being a woman. Her only instruction was in wearing high heels. 'There was no passing on of knowledge. She was just so tied up with whatever she was doing.'

* * *

Kate left Griffith High School in the summer of 1965. The end-of-year banquet made the cover of the *Area News*. The principal addressed the graduating class: 'I counsel particularly those going away from home to go to church. I also suggest you remember the debt you owe your home. Write home frequently and you cannot go wrong.'

Kate wasn't there as these words were spoken. She had already left.

She says she wrote against silences in her family history, exercised her imagination on them. 'I find solace in the thought that silence is something in itself, that it can have all kinds of attributes. It can be filled, and it can be broken ... The fear, of course, with my family history – and a parallel can be drawn with Australian history and culture – is that the silences were empty, that nothing much was going on.'

In an essay for *Vogue*, she did go back. There was a school reunion. 'They are irrigation babies,' she wrote, 'true children of progress.'

At Sydney University, Kate lived at Women's College. She stayed a year and hated it – 'way out of my depth, excruciatingly young and naïve, and with no social graces'. She says she 'took one look at the pearls-and-twinsetted Frensham girls … and realised I couldn't even begin to compete'.

She started to drink. She drank in binges and was guilty for it. She worked at David Jones and wrote poetry. 'I used to swan around in black velvet dress-shop dresses, half-pissed, and read these things. I was known for dire romances. A figure, shall we say.'

Always, she felt as if she didn't belong. 'I do remember several times men saying to me, "Why do you want to write? You're a woman." It was those times.'

* * *

Girlie has a skirt made of shot silk. She inspects it for pellet holes. Whenever a suitable song comes on the radio she races to put on the dress and dance around the kitchen. She twirls faster and faster. The spectacle appals Irene. Kate writes that of the many things about Girlie which irked Irene, this 'took the cake'.

The chapter is called 'Kangaroo Among the Beauty'. The line is from Emily Dickinson's first letters to Thomas Wentworth Higginson, the author and militant abolitionist. She was mostly unpublished at the time, writing to ask for reassurance, to see 'if my verse is alive?'

Higginson asked for her picture and instead Dickinson wrote him a description. She said she was small like a wren, with bold hair, her eyes like sherry left in a glass by a guest. She wrote: 'My business is circumference. An ignorance, not of customs, but if caught with the dawn, or the sunset see me, myself the only kangaroo among the beauty, sir, if you please, it afflicts me, and I thought that instruction would take it away.'

The chapter is Kate's favourite. She lets her fondness stray into the first person. 'To me, the key part of *Snake* is when Girlie is dancing. And her mother tells her to cut it out. I remember that skirt, the kitchen. I must have been about eight.'

*   *   *

The genius of *Snake* is its clarity. The story is small and everything. The silences, the ellipses of plot, are the holes families cut to make life bearable.

The book is written in arid prose, irrigated here and there with startling imagery. On every page it seems to suggest the same thing: Australia is a big country that makes sometimes small lives.

*   *   *

Every time I read *Snake*, I think it is about something else. One night I am convinced it is about a mother who loves her son so much she has her friend sleep with him.

We are told: 'Boy was exactly the child that Irene wanted, sturdily masculine, with a winning manner.' And: 'They enjoyed each other, mother and son. They laughed a lot.'

We are told: 'She knitted her lips, pained by everyone and everything, except for her beautiful blue-eyed Boy-o.'

We are told Irene has Boy sit with her as she bathes – 'soapy water lapping at her shoulders, legs bent so that her knees made islands, a flannel floating in the vicinity of her bosom for modesty's sake'. We are told that she does this 'even after Boy's voice broke and his body grew lanky'.

We are told the bathroom is cavelike and cool. Boy feeds a chip heater with slivers of pine. Boy and Irene recite snatches from *The Goon Show*. They are reciting a scene from *A Hard Day's Night* when, laughing, Irene's flannel slips. She is being Paul's grandfather and Boy is being Ringo. As her breast is exposed, Boy steals a glance. 'Irene knew he was looking; she rather enjoyed it,' Kate writes. 'How else was he to learn?'

It is Irene's friend Gwyneth who slips into Boy's bed and undoes the cord of his pyjamas. 'Not a word passed between them. Boy couldn't believe his luck.'

Afterwards, Irene says: 'How about that.'

The chapter is called 'A Laughing Woman with Two Bright Eyes'. The line is from 'The Temptations of St. Anthony', a comic song, first published in *Bentley's Miscellany* in 1838. The original goes:

Devils black and devils white,
Devils foolish, and devils wise;
But a laughing woman, with two bright eyes
Is the worsest devil of all.

It is hard, almost impossible, to say what *Snake* is really about. Kate's interpretation is this: it is about what happened. 'I wanted to make it everybody's story. Probably it is Dare's story the least, because he went off to agricultural boarding school. Poor, poor boy. I convinced him to go.'

I ask what she was thinking as she wrote. She pauses for a full minute, leaning forward and rubbing her palms against her eyes. 'Just how miserable it was, in our family. It was absolutely miserable. Really miserable. That's why in the first version she was the Wicked Witch. And I had to go back and fix that. I understand the reasons she was the way she was. She was like a car where the alarm's gone off and you can't turn it down. The lights – it's blaring and you can't stop it. And that was her whole life. She was truly, I don't know, beyond narcissistic. It was not just narcissism: it's something else. She came from a family of six people in Warrawee and her dad favoured her. She loved men. She really did light up like a Christmas tree when men were around.'

*   *   *

Hildegarde arrives on a motorcycle. Her surname is Hochschwender. Rex is happy Irene has a friend. The two women spend Saturday afternoons on the verandah listening to Liszt, Beethoven, Sibelius. Rex takes Hildegarde's advice on a gift to buy his wife and the forgiving look when Irene unwraps Mahler's *First* makes him feel momentarily not so useless.

Hildegarde ignores Boy but takes Girlie for burns on her motorbike. The four of them – Irene, Hildegarde, Boy and Girlie – go camping at a bend of the Murrumbidgee. After dark, Irene and Hildegarde undress and go down to the river. Later, a cow disturbs the tent where Girlie and Boy are sleeping. There are screams. Irene and Hildegarde come running, pulling on clothes as they go.

'That really happened,' Kate says. 'I mean, that *really* happened.' She says the word *really* in a way that makes her eyes bulge out. 'Mum was one for experimenting. Her reaction to that one was, "Well, I tried men so I thought I'd try women." Jesus, Mum.'

Kate says she remembers the tent. She remembers the cows coming down in the night to drink. 'The river was quite full. But they sort of barged into our tent. That is the first and last time I've gone camping.'

She checks with her brother. He remembers Hildegarde by name and bike: 'Thea Schmidt. Triumph motorcycle.'

* * *

Kate wrote *Snake* in four parts, but put almost all of the book into the third. The other sections fall off it, as if she has tried to peel a lemon with a broad knife. She wrote in different perspectives, but they were all her own. Occasionally, she addressed her characters as a conscience might.

A book of Kate's has never broken 200 pages. She calls them 'these sorts of books'. She says they are 'little half books'. She says 'they're lyric books but that doesn't mean they're lyrical'.

She says she doesn't know what to say about writing. When people ask, she tells them to prepare for a life of failure.

She keeps a clipping of a Weber cartoon. A young man is in his agent's office, the woman looking through his manuscript. The caption reads: 'Yep, that's it – seven pages. I only write what I know.'

Kate likens her own writing to painting, because she doesn't know what to say otherwise. She says impasto is the expression, but impasto is a bit thick. She mentions Whistler but she means Turner. 'Who does the big clouds?' she asks. 'I've got a book of them.'

She says Turner's pictures are actually quite grubby when you get close to them. She changes her mind: they're filthy. Whatever it is, she says, it's about building up parts and chopping off others and mostly chopping off others. 'There are too many words in the world,' she says. 'It's got to be exact.'

When she was writing *Snake*, an editor had to wrestle the manuscript off her. He said: 'Kate, give it to me. If you keep at it any longer, there won't be any book left.'

* * *

Kate believes her mother was mentally ill. Looking

back, Kate can't think specifically what the disorder might have been.

'She was trouble, that's all,' Kate says. 'As we would say in a country town: she was trouble.'

And again: 'I tried to think recently what was wrong with her. You could say she was a '50s beauty, but she was really in the wrong time. Too soon, I think. Maybe if she'd been back before the wars she would have had a better time.'

Kate was committed after she first attempted suicide. She had failed a year of university. She says she wasn't crazy: she just didn't know the size of the world yet.

'All I was – I wasn't crazy. I was just somebody who thought I would never fail. You know that feeling – that you'll always be okay. And I wasn't. It's something inside you. You've failed yourself.

So I just went back and increased my limit.'

*   *   *

The poem that ends Kate's first collection is called 'All of a Heap Anywhere, Megara, Megara'. The title references Sylvia Kantaris – legs apart, she wrote, in loneliness and desperation. The poem is Kate's exit, her escape. The year is 1975.

She wrote:

> *Kate Jennings, you could have become*
> *a daughter of*
> *the earth and the shadow*
> *but you knew the walls*
> *and the waiting would be the same.*

She wrote:

> *The only thing I wanted*
> *to remember was my mother,*

and that so, whenever
I found her
I could kill her.

*   *   *

Kate left on a scholarship to New York. She can't remember for how much.

She says her last months in Australia were horrible. She was living in Adelaide and hated it. In a letter, she wrote: 'I hate Adelaide'. She was supposed to be writing a novel, a feminist thriller. She had no money for meat, beer or real cigarettes.

'I'm scared of losing you too,' she wrote to a friend in a letter she never posted, 'but somewhere along the line I think I lost myself, which isn't a joke line … All I know is that I've never been so lonely and frightened.' Several months later, with a new ribbon in her typewriter, she continued: 'I've been unwell, lots of pills and more hospital. Something will have to give soon, just living in the past.'

Kate says this was a nothing period. She found it difficult to get out of bed. 'I was leaving. That's all. We wore ourselves out with politics in those houses and by the end of the '70s we had to get out.'

The book wasn't always called *Snake*. For a time it was *Goodbye to the Farm*.

* * *

Kate's jaw is her father's. She describes it as obstinate. She is correct. She wears on it her sets and her stubbornness. She holds on to slights. She is glamorous and you would call her beautiful. In an early draft of *Snake* she writes of 'this large jawed daughter'.

Kate has a craning neck, as if she is always trying to look over a neighbour's fence. Her limbs are long and gangly and in photographs it often seems as if she has collapsed in a heap. I think of the title of her first collection of stories, *Women Falling Down in the Street*. In a newspaper clipping she poses with a bob and hands like the twigs on an unlit fire. The headline is a quote from the article, written in bold text above the picture. It reads: 'Men are stupid.'

Kate is an expert in her own unhappiness. Sometimes, she is vinegar. She takes as her motto a line from Marie Bashkirtseff: 'Marry and have children? Any washerwoman can do that!'

For the back cover of her first poetry collection, she writes: 'Kate Jennings is a feminist. She believes in what Jane Austen recommended at fifteen: "Run mad as often as you chuse; but do not faint."'

Marie Bashkirtseff died at the age of twenty-five, slighted and suffering consumption. The same year, she had a painting in the Salon of a gang of young boys loitering on a street corner. It was praised but earned no medal. 'I am exceedingly indignant,' she wrote in her diary, 'because, after all, works that are really rather poor have received prizes … There is nothing more to be done. I am a worthless creature, humiliated, finished.'

In New York Kate lived in Hell's Kitchen. She was a horse loose in traffic. That's her phrase. She learnt to pray but not to God.

In her apartment, the floors were sloped and the bathroom was so small she had to step into the tub from one end. She saw a man stabbed and another man shot. Landlords burnt down their rent-controlled buildings. Twice she was robbed. 'People do come to New York to seek fame and fortune, but many more come to hide,' she wrote later. 'I dearly wanted to return to Australia, but I was too proud to go home with my tail between my legs.'

Kate says she writes for a kind of salvation. 'I don't think we're ever redeemed,' she says. 'I'm just trying to make sense of it all. I've had a good interesting life, but it has had its hard moments, and its heart-breaking moments, all the way through.'

She reflected once that 'the ways we relate to family can be as long-lived, insidious and difficult to uproot as couch grass'.

* * *

The fourth snake strikes a boy as he climbs over a log. The poison courses through him. The boy is in a film, being shown to Girlie's class. The narrator warns that the boy was careless. Australia, he says, has more poisonous snakes than any other continent. At night, Girlie imagines them, slithering up drainpipes and through knotholes.

Later, in a book on Australian fauna, she finds the pages feel as glossy as their scales might. Rex is skilled at killing them. He uses the sharp edge of a shovel.

* * *

The last time the police came, Kate had been drinking up and down 9th Street. Friends took her home but she broke away. She asked a friend to hug her and tell her she was alright. She was angry about couples. She called from bars, out of money. She hit someone. He hit her back. A barmaid was anxious for her. Two men carried her upstairs and she was held down on her bed.

A friend tried to restrain her, holding her, stroking her hair. She did this with difficulty. Someone called 911 and the process of hospitalisation was begun. Her friend warned Kate the police would come. She said Kate should not be frightened.

When the ambulance arrived, Kate became hysterical. They waited for the police. Kate was strapped to a stretcher.

She was admitted to the Bellevue. Once again, she was manacled. A medical student took down her history, as much as could be remembered. By now it was 8.30 a.m.

A friend recorded all this on a pad of yellow paper. In the left margin, she wrote: 'The suicidal tone – "I want to die" – became more strongly expressed as the evening wore on.'

Some time later, Kate wrote a poem called 'Desire'. She wrote: 'My outlook was as bitter as an unripe berry.' In the margin, she corrected herself: 'as tart as a quince'.

*   *   *

Kate doesn't know if her father read *Snake*. She doesn't know if her mother read it, either. Her brother, Dare, found it difficult. Recently, Kate says, he told her: 'I'm so glad you kept a record.'

Kate was once on a flight to Sydney with her cousin Shirley. She was touring the book about her border terriers, *Stanley and Sophie*. She calls it 'the dog book'. She says it was the best book tour she ever did because nobody got cross.

On the plane, Shirley said: 'I liked the recent book but, you know, I didn't care for any of the others.' Kate was tickled: 'That phrase – "I didn't care for any of the others" – was pretty wonderful.'

*   *   *

Kate lives sometimes in what she calls the black kelp of depression. She doesn't call it living, though: she calls it 'periods of entanglement'.

She lists Orwell, Beckett and Randall Jarrell as her favourite writers. 'Orwell and Jarrell for their straight-talking and their championing of clarity in language and lucidity in thought; Beckett for his paradoxical life-affirming nihilism.'

She says: 'I find it easier to write novels than to

inhabit Janet Malcolm's famous "House of Actuality".'

She once wrote this line, about the Front Lawn Speech she made at a moratorium in Sydney, the speech that called for women to arm themselves and rise up against men: 'There is something in my make-up that ups the ante, instinctively going all out to reject you if I sense you will reject me.'

* * *

When Kate was ninety days sober, she wrote a letter to herself. She said she was 'pleased, happy to be a part of AA'. She said the remarkable thing about AA was that she had accepted it. 'This is what I have to be, what I want to be. And thank goodness, at long last, that I'm here.'

She said for the first time she was not thinking too hard, not trying to control everything. 'Of course, I get cross, mad, angry, bored, and I want to drink. I want to drink when I'm feeling rotten or anxious, but even more, I want to drink when I'm feeling good.'

She missed the hangovers. She missed the days in bed, full up on sleeping tablets, when her head stopped. She found it hard to share stories in the meetings. She missed oblivion. In a different pen, she wrote: 'It's easier to be sick than to start the process; it's easier to be guilty than responsible.'

Partway through the letter, she offered a brief biography, as she might at a meeting:

'I grew up in the country in NSW, Australia. My father is a farmer. My mother, a very bright beautiful woman, married him because he was a handsome soldier who could dance well.

'No drinking at home; the odd sherry. I did have an uncle who drank. My mother was pretty crazy, though. All this energy and nothing to do with it.

'I grew up awkward, gangly, freckles, reinforced by mother. I became bookish – that well-worn path to being alcoholic. I wanted to be a beatnik poet. I did grow up to be a writer and a poet.

'University – difficulty in getting through. That first bottle of vodka/valium ...'

She wrote about shock treatment, about becoming a feminist. Her thoughts jumbled out of order. She was in and out of hospital. She mentioned jail. She wrote: 'I did things I would not have done if I had not been drinking.' She wrote: 'Lying dormant – on that floor and these two black labradors trying to maul me.'

By the end of the letter she was making only jottings: 'America – a journey of self-discovery.' And: 'Bellevue – depression.' And, finally: 'One drink and would be crazy.'

* * *

The car accident happens a mile from home. Girlie is lightly hurt. Irene is trapped under the car, unconscious, covered in blood and dust. Her necklace is biting into her neck, and Girlie tries to free it. As she does, blood bubbles from her mother's mouth. 'An idea detonated in Girlie's mind,' Kate writes: 'she had killed her mother, choked her. Girlie's hands fell to her sides.'

In her notes on an earlier draft, Kate wrote: 'Wants mother dead. Car accident tune changes to wants herself dead.'

Later, she wrote: 'The car accident. She has killed her mother … from then on she turns it on herself. She is the one who will die … She grows into an adult with a fierce desire for death.'

Kate allowed Irene one last boast, absent from the final draft: 'In the ambulance she says we shall see the Queen.'

* * *

There is a box Kate keeps of letters from old lovers. They are wet with the anguish of romance felt unequally.

One begins: 'I didn't like your suicide note.'

Another ends: 'I love you, Kate, and I'm scared of the sort of love I think you have for me, and the lack of it for yourself.'

* * *

Kate started writing letters to publishers in New York, announcing her intentions. She said she would write a series of category romances. In one letter she announced that she would write one set in the magazine business in New York and another set in Peru. She crossed out the second suggestion.

In the same letter she wrote, 'my training is as a poet and critic – with tendency towards brevity and succinctness – so I am laboriously teaching myself to be more fulsome'. To prove the point, she went back and removed the extraneous 'and succinctness'.

The letter finished: 'If I ever have the time and money, I plan to write two "big" books, one with the precious stones world as a background, the other a mother–daughter saga set in Australia and the United States. I have enclosed synopses of these, and I am currently working on chapter outlines.'

In a letter to a friend, written at the same time, she wrote: 'I am determined to succeed – as an editor and a writer – and not lose my heart to foolish, cowardly men. AA tries to teach you to become a nicer person … but it's going to be uphill for me. But I'm working on it.'

* * *

As Kate wrote *Snake*, she referred back to an entry in Hugh Rawson's *Wicked Words*. She calls it a 'marvellously idiosyncratic book'.

The entry offered the etymology of various phrases using the word *snake*. It canvassed Shakespeare and Aesop, the snake that bit the farmer's bosom. It offered the Roman *snake in the grass*.

It considered the low slang, and asked the reader to 'see also *schlong*'. It defined a *snake* as a young woman, perhaps because of her treacherous nature, who at college lived in a *snake house* and who in a brothel might call it a *snake ranch*. Men were also *snakes*, or *parlour snakes*.

Snake juice was whisky, as was *snake medicine* and *snake poison*. The source of these was drunkenness, or *seeing snakes*. An insane asylum was a *snake pit*, probably for the same reason.

To *snake* was to cheat. *To be snakebit* was to be injured or jinxed. A *snake story* was long and convoluted and ultimately unbelievable. *To wake snakes* was to get into trouble, but *to kill snakes* was to mind your own business. *Snake oil*, finally, was a misrepresentation. The entry concluded with the advice, 'See also *adder, deaf as an*; *copperhead*; *rattlesnake*; and *viper*.'

Kate says she liked the way the meanings criss-crossed and tangled. Some were at odds with others. 'None of the meanings were without malice,' she said. 'And so I tried to hold the book together with that idea. Can't say anybody noticed or even mentioned snakes literally or metaphorically.'

*   *   *

Dare has soft features. His words come out padded, like bolls of cotton. He looks like Kate and she looks like him.

The childhood he remembers was normal. Kate was introverted, bookish. Sometimes, she was mean. At fourteen she decided she wanted to be a beatnik. He was twelve and all he knew was that he didn't want to be a farmer.

'There were times when everything was tense,' he says. 'There were other times where everything was funny and normal. My mother was certainly highly strung and incredibly unhappy. I guess you would say that was the problem. It wasn't the happiest household but it wasn't terrible either.'

He remembers a house full of books and music. His mother gave them that. She wanted to travel, to go to the Greek islands. After the car accident, she used the insurance payout for her fare. Dare is sure she enjoyed the handsome young men. When she came back, the lamb was always served with feta. Dare says her name: Edna.

'My mother never read the book, because she knew what it was,' he says. 'But she always read the *Bulletin* from cover to cover. And the *Bulletin* did a review of it. And the first line of the review was, "This book is remarkable for depicting one of the most despicable women in Australian literature." Or something like that. Poor thing: she cried for a month.'

*   *   *

Kate made notes as she wrote, not bothering to stop, her page becoming a kind of half-formed poem. A paragraph would end, and then the points would begin. She wrote: 'Think up more things for boy.' And: 'Brother and sister rivalry.'

These points became lists, reordered with each draft: 'Her clothes/The last lover. The Murrumbidgee/The car accident, how she thinks she has killed her mother/Changes in the house, the phone down the wall/Sessions listening to music the absolute ecstasy of it/The photographer lover.'

The spelling was urgent, eccentric: 'Seesions lsitening to msuci the abssltue ewctasy of it.'

She makes notes for a version of the book she never writes. 'You might want to know what happened,' she begins. 'Rex met a woman who liked him. They never married but spent whatever time they could together, went on holidays. They held hands, giggled, chattered like two noisy birds in a tree.

'Irene made the same mistake all over again. She remarried a man who was wiry and sexy. Like Rex he wasn't educated; she would change him, she would change him. He was more of a bully, called her at her tricks, upstaged her, and so a balance: she met her match.

'Boy became a man with no trouble at all; he never made peace with his father. He never married, either. He is wary about women, like a hunter in a jungle where ...' The thought doesn't finish, instead it repeats: 'Weariness when he is around women.'

And of herself: 'Girlie is a mess; in her world there is always snakes coming up the pipes, feathers to be collected, colour pencils to be envied.'

*   *   *

Rex leaves his dog in the car and she dies. There is a mouse plague. Then a dust storm. Then a plague of locusts. Then hail.

Irene takes work with a photographer in town. He gives her a necklace. She gives it back, says it is inappropriate.

The chapter has the make of an affair. The book lives on small details.

*   *   *

Dare says there was no Gwyneth to sneak into his bed. 'Yeah, I wish,' he says. 'I remember there was one of Mum's friends, and she was a terrible flirt. But no – it was never consummated.'

The cavelike bathroom was really a drum outside. 'We had this huge tank with a big hose coming out of it. Mum and Dad and I would also go and wash under it in the nude. But Cathy wouldn't, because she was too shy … My mother – she was very casual about nudity. It wasn't a big deal.'

Dare says the trouble with books is that if a little bit is real, all of it becomes real. No one wants to accept it can be both. 'And it is really hard – when somebody writes about you, you feel so defenceless. You can't defend yourself, that's the worst thing about it.'

He remembers the same mother Kate does, although he remembers her differently. They had a very different relationship. It was warm, close.

'The fact was, my mother was a big city girl: very

pretty, very vivacious. Loved men. Loved her life,' he says. 'Dad was a tall, handsome but probably fairly dull wheat farmer from Temora. She'd just come out of the Second World War, when Sydney was awash with handsome Americans and all of that. Apparently she almost married an American. There was always a Fifth Air Force shoulder patch in her drawer. These weird things that you see.'

He says: 'My first name is Alan. Not my given name. I don't know why – Dare is a name from my father's side. But Alan is my first name. According to my sister, and I don't know if this is true, that's the name of the American. So you could see there was a lot of, kind of, unhappiness there.'

*   *   *

Kate met Bob on a magazine. She does not remember the title. She had been sober a year, 'which is huge'.

She was a proofreader, although she was no good

at it. She says people liked her and she hung on wherever she hung on. She says New York was full of women her age carrying around copies of *The Chicago Manual of Style*.

Bob was a designer. He had lost his money and was working on refreshing a handful of magazines. Kate says he was swindled. She didn't know anything about him but he was the closest person to her when she got the clipping of a poem she had published in the *Sydney Morning Herald*. 'I was pleased as punch,' she says.

Kate was smiling when she showed it to him. He liked the poem. They started to talk.

'The thing about Bob was, he was so nice,' Kate says. 'He was the nicest man I've met. And I'd only ever, ever gone out with shits. The nastier they were … don't quote me. They had to be handsome; they had to be bad choices.'

I t was a school friend who told Kate. They were sitting beside the river in New York, forty years after they graduated from Griffith High School. She said, 'What about your mum and Mr Tasker?' Kate said, 'What about Mum and Mr Tasker?' Her friend said, 'You didn't know?'

Kate was furious. The rage lasted days.

'I knew a couple of people she was screwing but not Mr Tasker, my primary-school teacher,' she said. 'I got really, really upset at the age of sixty-something. I called Dare and said, "Did you know this?" And Dare laughed and laughed and laughed. And he said, "Cathy, Mum was flirting with the male nurses right until the very end." That's what she was.'

* * *

Late in the book Irene becomes a writer. It is a source of tension with the narrator. She becomes a humorist, or fancies she is one, writing a column on farming life for the local paper. Betty MacDonald is her model. The pieces are rueful and upbeat. When neighbours ask, Rex says they are a bit rich.

'Mum had a typewriter,' Kate says. 'She wanted to be a writer. She actually did get something published in the newspaper and they cut it for length and that was the end of her writing. I don't know.'

* * *

The first rejection came from Picador. The editor there was Reagan Arthur. 'As discussed, and with real regret, I'm returning here Kate Jennings' novella *Snake*, along with the copies of her earlier books that you had kindly furnished. I think she's just a lovely writer, and I found something sort of cinematic in *Snake*; she manages to convey a great deal of atmosphere and menace and suspense in such a short amount of time. And clearly she's a writer with good work behind her and more to come, so I like the idea of getting in on the (American) ground floor. Unfortunately, other readers found it too elliptical and a little harder to warm up to or see how we could sell this effectively, and without any other support I don't have much room to make it work here.'

The next came six weeks later, from Henry Holt and Company. 'I liked *Snake* but I don't see much I can do with it. Jennings has a nice clean style and I'd be happy to see more of her work – but this just is not something I feel I can go out with and get much attention for.'

The letters kept on like this, warm but inert. Kate is good, they said, but she has no market.

*   *   *

Kate keeps clippings on writing. She clips an article

from *HQ* magazine, titled 'It's Your Life (And I'll Write about It If I Want to)'. She puts highlighter over a line about the 'ruthlessness of the creative person'. Further on, she runs her pen under a quote from Andrew McGahan: 'If you use your friends in any way you see fit, then the books may be better, but you can't expect to be accepted. I'd rather have friends.'

She clips a full-page feature from the *New York Times*, folding it once and then again. The piece is called 'My Mother and I Don't Speak Anymore'.

* * *

Boy tries to kill the snake with an axe. He chases it the length of the front path, bringing down the blade, leaving a line of regular gouges in the concrete.

In the next chapter, a snake comes by Girlie as she walks to the vegetable garden. Her father tries to kill it, without success. Irene is bemused.

* * *

The rejection letters went into a folder with the others she received for her essay collection and her short stories. They are battlefield souvenirs of the war that is writing – shell casings collected and kept to prove wrong.

There is Simon & Schuster: 'She does have the wonderfully honest one-two punch of a feminist, along with the entirely receptive curiosity that I think is quite Australian (and very endearing). I don't think we could really do justice to these essays if we published them here, though.'

The *New Yorker*: 'We're sorry to say that this submission isn't quite right for us, in spite of its evident merit.' And then by hand: 'Please try us again. Thanks.'

There is St Martin's Press: 'I can see why you're keen on the essays: they're well observed, witty, and thoughtful. But they did feel to me, somehow, slight, with the ephemeral quality of journalism about them … I liked the stories better, I guess because they were less journalistic, but they too had a sketchy feel about them, as though they had started out as essays and not gotten all the way to being stories yet.'

And Random House: 'I think she is writing too frequently for an Australian audience to make these viable as a collection for us, but of course I'd be glad to consider a proposal … I don't have any brilliant ideas for her, as she writes best about exile, and you need a special take on the topic to produce a saleable book.'

* * *

Kate says the first poem she wrote after meeting Bob was the long poem about Martin Johnston, called 'Without Preamble'. It is an angry, sad poem about getting sober and being ignored. It is a poem of greatness sidestepped with drink, a poem of walking skeletons.

She sees Johnston's writing, dense with allusion. By contrast, her poems bristle 'unfashionably with declarative sentences'. He was lauded, Kate writes. She was laughed at. 'Too much was asked of you,' Kate writes. 'The reverse/is true for me: I am a farmer's daughter.'

She drank in fits and let the shame chase her into foxholes. He drank to stay drunk. She left Australia to stop, to dry out with no one watching.

Partway through the poem she found her conclusion: 'you are dead, and I was nearly so'.

The dates are wrong. Kate had been with Bob a decade by the time Johnston died and she wrote the poem. But the sentiment is the same: the poem is about finding one's place, and she found it with Bob.

'Nobody encouraged me,' Kate says. 'This is the amazing thing about my life, looking back. Nobody encouraged me. Mum didn't encourage me. Dad didn't. None of my family. No teacher did. Nobody at high school or university. That's why I wrote the Martin Johnston poem. I met my husband here and he encouraged me. He said, "You can do it." It took a long while to find somebody who would say, "You're okay in your own skin, and you can write."'

'Without Preamble' ends Kate's second collection of poetry. She dedicates the book to her husband. She writes: 'For Bob Cato.'

* * *

Every night as she worked on *Snake* she read to Bob what she had written that day. It was the last book she wrote this way. He was diagnosed with Alzheimer's disease four years before *Snake* came out. She put it in a drawer.

'I know I put it away for a while. And I'm glad I did. I made it a lot better, so Mum wasn't ... so much.

I wrote most of it before I went to banks, which was much earlier. It was after that book of essays, which Penguin made such a balls-up of. They didn't proofread it and they put the wrong laminate on the cover or something.'

Kate took a job on Wall Street, to pay for Bob's care. She became a speechwriter. She was working at J.P. Morgan or Merrill Lynch when the book came out. She can't remember which. The publisher was Ecco.

*   *   *

As an adult, Kate does not shy from embarrassments. If anything, she treats them as a virtue. She begins an essay, 'I have no money and neither does Bob.'

It is a schoolgirl's trick: point out the worst before someone else can. She realised early there was no point trying to pass. She meant socks that were elasticised rather than turned over, shoes that were the right brown, and legs scrubbed hairless with abrasive mitts. 'I wanted more than anything else never to appear foolish; but suffering the usual torment of a tall, flat-chested girl growing up in a country town, I decided that it was better to be deliberately unfashionable and outrageous than to fit in.'

Later, she says: 'I don't care about being embarrassed. We've all been young. I'm always going to be twelve years old. I refuse to be anything else.'

*   *   *

The review in the *Bulletin* was by Elizabeth Riddell. The piece was headed 'Desperately Seeking Satisfaction'. The first sentence was: 'What astonishment, stimulation, refreshment, enjoyment is to be found in this short novel – 145 pages, and some of these are half-pages only – by Kate Jennings, known to many of us as a poet and collector of other people's poetry, some of it under the inglorious title of *Mother I'm Rooted.*'

Riddell wrote that the book was not about a snake, except now and then. It was about Irene. 'Irene was not interested in sex,' she wrote, 'but in power. She exercised great power, affectionately disguised, on Rex and on the two children, unfortunately called Girlie and Boy.'

Later, she wrote: 'Bored of Rex and Girlie, and kept at a distance by Boy, Irene tries everything on offer in the town and district – baking scones, playing bridge, working at the radio station and the photographer's, stray men, a lesbian intruder, do-gooding. She endures dust storms, droughts, floods, locust and mouse plagues. She turns her back by day and night on Rex. In the end, he is not much worse off than he was on the day he married her. His only retaliatory action has been to hurl the lesbian from the house.'

Towards the end of the review, she wrote: 'Reviewers must beware of telling the plot.'

*   *   *

A friend suggested she leave Bob. 'You know, you don't have to do this,' she said. 'You're still young.' Kate looked at her, appalled: 'He's my family.'

In the visitors' book at the hospice, Kate's name appeared every day. Occasionally, she left him notes, reminders for a brain that could not remember. 'Kate is in Australia!' she wrote. 'Visiting her dad. She will be back on March 17. Two weeks!'

She circled the last two words and drew a love heart, the top stretched out like the Gulf of Carpentaria. The bottom looped around and looked almost like Tasmania.

In the visitors' book, Bob drew pictures of her. Her neck was long, framed by hair. He drew her lips full but her smile was unconvinced. His pen became halting and the ink made little pools along the course of his line. Occasionally, he ran out of time. Her face was left empty: brows, a nose, a chin, but no eyes to see and no mouth to speak.

A year before he died, Kate wrote a short email to a friend named Susan: 'Boy, am I depressed. I also have a cold. I dreamed last night that I went on a rampage and then swam out to sea and drowned myself. The mind is wonderfully clichéd. I got the additional info for the Medicaid people (market value of the studio), and now I just have to wait to see what they will demand. Then I hire a lawyer.'

*   *   *

Carol Shields reviewed the book for the *New York Times*. The piece was startlingly positive. In *Snake*'s brief chapters, she found 'a poet's shorthand, perhaps, or a magician's spell'. She said the narrative was 'stunning'. The spare scenes caught the 'absolute rub of the quotidian' and 'possess what feels like a holographic shimmer'. The review finished: 'American readers will feel themselves fortunate to make the acquaintance of a writer like Kate Jennings.'

Publishers Weekly was just as enthusiastic: 'Domestic dystopia has rarely been distilled into such concentrated literary form … This snake of a novel is lethal and fast-moving – and so spare it will leave readers wishing for more.'

The day of the *Times* notice Kate was not angry at Bob's unwell brain. Several times she told him that she got a good review and several times he said how wonderful that was. It pleased her to hear it. 'It was a fabulous review,' she said. 'This is what you dream of.'

After breakfast, she pushed his wheelchair in Central Park. Her jeans caught in the spokes and she tripped.

She lay flat on her back and stared up at the blue day.

* * *

In an early draft of 'Deserta Rerum', the poem that wasn't working, she let sentiment catch on snags of contempt. She wrote of a life 'full of sour Australian indifference'. The paddocks were 'scarified by heartbreak'. She played Patience with her grandmother, learnt to knit loose stitches like the slack underlip of a cow. But this, she wrote, was nostalgia. 'There is nothing left but pessimism.' The line was cut by the next draft. So was this one: 'Nothing, in the end, is ever forgiven.'

She mentioned her father's dancing, said it was why her mother married him. He was tall and handsome in a uniform. Then a thought, sectioned off in brackets:

I have recounted
this so often in making sense of my story to

whoever
would listen that it is almost not true,
and yet there is evidence, a pair of men's dancing
pumps
in a musty shoe cupboard, the kid leather creased
into a maze of crazed lines, so soft,
I would put one to my cheek and rub, and wonder.

This uncertainty of memory did not survive the next edit.

*   *   *

Kate writes close to life. Not completely close, she says. She does make up things. 'I round the corners,' she says, 'and make the really ghastly stuff a little better.'

She went to a bookstore to watch Jamaica Kincaid reading. 'Somebody asked her if her books were autobiographical. Stupid question. And she said, "Every comma, every period, is autobiographical."'

Kate made notes for a speech she had to give about *Snake*. They were bullet points, underlined and crossed out in pencil, or else hemmed off in scratchy rectangles.

She wrote: 'What's curious about *Snake* is how everybody reads it differently. In a single day, I had someone say to me that it was about a mother and a daughter; another, that it was about a brother and a sister; yet another, an unhappy marriage. All those things, I would have thought, but none exclusively.'

Kate wrote that the book was about three major themes. The first was the 'loneliness of men married to unkind women'. The second was how the unloved become unlovable. The third, she wrote, was the flow of culture: how a little house in the middle of nowhere could be a magnet for everything from George Seferis to *The Pajama Game*. She wrote that the emotions were autobiographical but not necessarily the story.

In another point, heavily marked, she wrote: 'Unsentimental. One thinks of *Thelma and Louise* – only in this case the female protagonist just drives off to another life.'

* * *

Bob was an art director and vice president of creative services for CBS-Columbia Records. He collaborated with Robert Rauschenberg and Andy Warhol. He won Grammys for his work with Bob Dylan and Barbra Streisand. He gave Janis Joplin the title *Cheap Thrills* for her second record and chose Robert Crumb to illustrate the sleeve.

Bob died on 19 March 1999. His obituary in the *New York Times* called him a 'ground-breaking graphic designer who helped turn the record album cover into an important form of contemporary art'.

It continued: 'The cause was complications of Alzheimer's disease, said his wife, Kate Jennings.'

Kate is generous. She insists on sending presents. She defends friendships and tends them with unexpected kindnesses. 'Why not?' she says. 'I love giving people presents.'

She sends a copy of Janet Kauffman's story collection *Obscene Gestures for Women* and Lorine Niedecker's *Blue Chicory* and Djuna Barnes's *The Book of Repulsive Women*. She sends a small silver head of a bodhisattva with an instruction that it is to be worn on leather as a necklace. She sends a stone amulet in a Thistle & Bee box and a first edition of Claud Cockburn's autobiography, *A Discord of Trumpets*.

Kate speaks as if the sentences have suddenly occurred to her. The words are firm but her voice is singsong. I ask about her childhood and she replies that she is watching *Taboo*. 'Tom Hardy is delicious.'

She is easily exasperated, at least for comic effect. 'Hey,' she says, 'that's my story and I'm sticking to it.' Sometimes, she says: 'I'm so bossy.'

As I write this essay, her names for me are: 'kiddo', 'sweetie-pie' and 'silly old possum'.

*   *   *

Twice after Bob died, Kate went to a therapist. 'I sat there and cried and said, "Oh, no. Oh, no. I'm sorry, I'm sorry, I'm sorry."'

Immediately, she started writing *Moral Hazard*. It was a novel of their final years together. 'I had to tie myself to the chair to write the Bob parts,' she said. 'I cried the whole way through, while I was writing. But it would have been for nought if I hadn't got that story down. That's all.'

At the end of *Moral Hazard* the wife character gives her sick husband a drink of Nantucket Nectars.

Mixed in are the pills that will kill him. 'I don't remember what I then said or did, how long I sat with him,' Kate writes. 'I probably kissed him, told him how much I loved him.'

*   *   *

Her mother moved to Red Valley, to an outpost wrecked by monsoon and sunlight. There was a pub, an abattoir and a caravan park. Kate went decades without seeing her. Dare finally persuaded a meeting. 'We had never got on well, and for much longer than was appropriate I blamed her for my shortcomings … It was time to get on with my own dying.'

Kate's mother was two hours late to pick her up in Katherine. Kate held out her hand in greeting; her mother hugged her. Edna had taken up with a man from the Darlington Point Bowling Club. He worked as a yardsman and she was a cook. Eventually, they ran a tourist boat together.

Kate stayed for three days. On the flight back she sat next to a policeman from Tennant Creek and cried at the waste and selfishness. He looked deeply embarrassed.

'I never reconciled with her. I never bothered. I couldn't. If you go thirty years without speaking to somebody, you've got a good reason. The minute you get near her, she's like kryptonite. She starts undermining you. She just does. She's got this … It's just horrible.'

The last words Kate said to her mother were: 'If you ever have another child, don't tell them they're ugly. Tell them they're beautiful, even if they aren't.'

* * *

Kate finds *Snake* difficult to read. 'I do go back to it every year and make sure that I did the right thing. I had to think it through,' she says. 'I had a hard time reading it. I just got sadder and sadder.

It did make me very sad. I can only call it sad. I felt sad for the mother, sad for me. Sad for Dad. Very sad for Dad.'

She says the book is not about revenge. She doesn't believe in it. 'That whole catharsis thing – I hate that. I do the same thing that you do: I write to work out what I think. And I wrote it to work out what I thought. And there it is. I hate that psycho-analytic crap. For heaven's sakes, writing is really hard. I don't get it out of my system, that's for sure. I don't say, "There you go." At any time things can come boiling up and hit me that I thought I'd stowed away years ago.'

Kate keeps filing cards with notes written on them. One says: 'I can never, it seems at times, escape from that family's failures. I can never, it seems at times, recover/get over from the failure of that family.'

Another says: 'Maybe it doesn't matter anymore

who said what to whom during childhood. The real question is, how did one grow up?'

On the second card, she has crossed out the word *maybe* and the word *anymore*.

* * *

Kate went back to visit the farm, just to check. The house was pulled down. The woolshed, wet with lanolin, was collapsing like a soufflé. A child with a full nappy was bouncing on his mother's knee. The burrs on the banks of the channels had been left to grow. Kate said the people who owned the farm were subhuman. Somehow, she said, they had got rich. 'The only thing left was a silky oak. Mum planted a silky oak.'

* * *

There was encouragement. There were fierce friendships with Helen Garner and Drusilla Modjeska and others. Cards came, and letters. On 10 May

1975, there was one from Garner. Kate was living at 117 St Johns Road, Glebe. The card showed Orcagna's *Inferno*, a detail from *The Last Judgment*, of a devil woman preying on a soldier. The script was printed, almost childlike:

> Dear Kate, this morning I have the sad task of cleaning out Falconer Street. I'm doing my room and I swore I wouldn't read anything, only work, but I picked up your 'Melancholy' poems and read the one that ends 'I was ugly in the sunlight' and my eyes got full of the old tears of knowledge and familiarity. You've got a job to do, Kate, don't drop your bundle! Or your sword or your pen. Yr loving friend Helen. P.S. Alice has mumps.

* * *

Books get lost. Someone once told me they are like yoghurt: the shelf life is fourteen days, and then they are gone.

Snake was lost. 'It was pretty well ignored,' Kate says.

She blames the feminism from which she is descended. She says: 'They're real bitches, some of those women.' She says they couldn't accept the treatment she gave her mother, the way she wrote a woman as unfeeling. 'You're not supposed to do that.'

In the *Sydney Morning Herald*, Debra Adelaide spent much of her review quarrelling with the book's cover lines. 'I'm afraid my breath was not taken, not once,' she wrote. 'Nor did I feel heat or smell disillusionment; or smell anything, unless it was the odour of new paper.'

Later, she conceded the merit of its tension. 'What sets *Snake* apart from the run of the mill is its scrupulous clarity of purpose: what could be a long family saga is told within a very short space, and the landscape, the characters, the events are at their most succinct and vivid.'

When the book was re-released seven years later, the *Age* said it was 'probably the most accomplished, realistic novel about bush life to be produced in the past decade'.

Snake failed to find an audience. It never had a good cover. Its subject was unfashionable. Several times it was described as a descendant of Henry Lawson's short story 'The Drover's Wife'.

Its failure is less complicated, however. The fact is this: *Snake* is too small. Little books are pushed out into the world and then they die. A midwife would call it failure to thrive.

* * *

Dare offered to read *Snake* to his father, to make it easier. His father declined. He found the material too difficult.

'It was very mean, to my mother,' Dare says. 'You

know, first novels settle scores. I'm easily recognisable as the vacuous younger sibling. You know, my father is the confused, decent bloke, not understanding what's going on. I was conflicted: it was so beautifully written and wonderfully depicted, but I knew everyone in there.'

He says his mother was always proud of Kate's writing. He says at one level she took credit for it. He picks up a copy of *Snake* and begins to read from the first page. His voice lingers proud around the words.

'She is your wife, she despises you,' he reads. 'The coldness, the forbearing looks, the sarcastic asides, they are constant. She emasculates you with the sure blade of her contempt. The whirring of the whetstone wheel, the strident whine of steel being held to it, that is the background noise to the nightmare of your days.'

He stops for a moment, his eyes crinkling into a

smile. 'I mean, that's pretty fucking good.'

* * *

Early drafts of *Snake* carried different epigraphs.

Initially, Kate chose Elizabeth Bishop and Samuel Beckett.

She quoted Bishop:

> *Goodbye to the elms,*
> *to the farm, to the dog.*
> *The bus starts. The light*
> *grows richer; the fog,*
> *shifting, salty, thin,*
> *comes closing in.*

And Beckett: 'The memory came faint and cold of the story I might have told, a story in the likeness of my life, I mean without the courage to end or the strength to go on.'

Then it was *Antony and Cleopatra*: 'Thou shouldst come like a Fury crown'd with snakes.' And Henry Green: 'You know Bert I sometimes marvel women can go sour like that. When you think of them young, soft and tender it doesn't 'ardly seem possible now the way they turn so that you would never hold a crab apple up to them they're so acid.'

In the end she settled on just one, a verse of Elizabeth Riddell's:

> *When the dog at morning*
> *Whines about the frost*
> *I shall be in another place.*
> *Lost, lost, lost.*

* * *

Kate's mother wrote a letter from her deathbed. She was seventy-two. It was melanoma. 'I thought she'd be around forever. But, no: seventy-two.'

Kate read the letter then put it aside. It said: 'I believe you've done well for yourself. In my next life, I will, too. I will be a writer.' Kate didn't answer. 'In some other life she's going to be a writer,' she said, 'and she's going to be famous and all that stuff?'

Later, Kate was sitting in an AA meeting. The woman beside her was crying. 'Her mother had died and she loved her mother. And I looked at her and I could not believe there was a woman sitting there who loved her mother. That's how alien it was to me.'

* * *

I saw Kate once more on that first trip, for coffee at the Lincoln Center.

I cut through Central Park and listened as a rickshaw driver told two German tourists about the Bethesda Fountain. 'This is a symbol of the city, a monument to New York,' he said. 'It was also used as a location in *Home Alone 2.*'

America is a land of unintended bathos. There is no distinction here between the ridiculous and the sublime.

Kate wrote about this fountain in an essay she named for the last words said by the first American gassed on death row. Over and over, as the pellet dropped into the chamber and poison filled the room, he said: 'Save me, Joe Louis. Save me, Joe Louis.'

She wrote about the porridge humidity of summer and the faces worthy of Breughel and what she called the park's ersatz pastorality. New York is cruel in her stories and she is cruel to it.

I was early and stopped for a shoeshine. I would never usually but this was only my second time in New York and I was dumb with affection. I was wearing the same threadbare jacket.

Kate talked about the poet Frederick Seidel, and other names I did not recognise. She quoted his line: 'A naked woman my age is just a total nightmare.'

Nervous, I said, 'Yes.' I said it when she mentioned other writers: Philip Levine, Wallace Stevens, James Fenton. I said it on the leeside of her thoughts, a kind of anxious punctuation.

Eventually, she paused and looked at me. Her eyes had a disappointed intensity. 'Are you saying that because you understand?' she said. 'Or because you don't understand?'

*   *   *

The last years of Kate's father's life he spent with a woman called Beth. They held hands and talked like pigeons. He had never really spoken to his children, was embarrassed by his lack of education. When Kate came home to visit, he drove her to the Darlington Point Bowling Club. There was silence when they entered. He signalled to the band. They had one dance and left, father and daughter. 'It says something about him. Mum was meeting this guy there and going down to the banks of the Murrumbidgee with a towel. I mean, really.'

Kate's father did not go to Beth's funeral. He hated crowds. He never visited her grave. He said he was waiting for the headstone. 'That's so typical of Dad,' Kate said. 'No tears or nothing, just matter-of-fact: "I'll wait for that."'

The final thing he did, as Kate walked across the car park of his nursing home at Coleambally, was raise his arm and give a tight salute. It was the last time Kate saw him. 'It's an army thing,' Kate said. 'In that context, it meant, "That's it, kiddo. We did what we did."'

*   *   *

When Irene leaves, Rex says nothing. He thinks

about shooting her and then himself. He watches from the kitchen table and then the garden as her car passes across the landscape, behind box trees and over bridges, until it is gone.

He walks the property for five days, circling it, crossing its paddocks, following the fence lines. Sleepless and starving, he decides God is walking with him.

He burns Irene's things in an incinerator. Her records form a single ugly lump. He buys two hundred pigs and starts drinking. The pigs devour Irene's irises, grubbing out the rhizomes from the earth. Six months to the day after she left, he drives his car into the Murrumbidgee River. He does not leave a note.

The same thing happened to a wool classer when Kate was a child – a man she liked, who told her long story poems. 'One year he didn't show up and what had happened was his wife ran off with somebody

and he got in his car and went into the Murrumbidgee. People do that sort of thing out there. They
drown themselves – and their children – in dams.'

Kate says that if she had been her father she would
have shot herself or driven into a river. It was only
on re-reading the book that she remembered she
had Rex do the same.

Irene sings show tunes as she drives away. Her
hands are trembling. She moves north and finds
a new partner. She decides that the figure with
whom she most identifies is Oscar Wilde, exiled
and pilloried. She takes to quoting Hippocrates'
first aphorism: 'Life is short, and the Art long;
the occasion fleeting; experience deceitful, and
judgment difficult.'

Without indicating that she has done so, Kate
scratches from the sentence its second clause. She
refuses Irene any mention of creativity, any of the

art that might survive her. She gives her only brevity and confusion. This is how the great Australian novel ends.

One Saturday, I ask Kate what made her a writer. There is a long and painful pause. An unhappy knowledge settles on her face. 'Probably, it was Mum.'

EPILOGUE

Kate lives in a house of ghosts. Everyone is there except Bob. She saw him die and mourned him while he was alive.

The first ghost she saw was her paternal grandmother. It was on 48th Street. 'She did appear,' Kate says, 'and it amazed me that she was so traditionally a ghost.' In a poem, Kate says she was soft around the edges and alive with a sweet glow. The ghost told Kate she had gone a long way but not far enough.

When Kate's mother died there was a huge blizzard. Dare organised a wake in Sydney. Kate didn't go. Dare says the wake was full of women who told him his mother had inspired them. 'She had travelled, she had lived,' he says. 'She was a decent woman.'

Kate could feel her mother's presence and walked through the snow to a church on the Upper East Side. She had to bang on the door to be let in. Crying and aloud, she said: 'Mum, go away. Stop lurking.'

Kate was less surprised when her father appeared. He had been there her entire life. During Bob's sickness, he phoned once a week. The calls lasted two minutes and meant the world. When Laurence Jennings died, he stayed on, present as the telephone.

'I wake up in the morning and I think they're all there in the room next door,' Kate says. 'I think that's called grieving.'

ACKNOWLEDGEMENTS

This essay is for Kate Jennings. It is a love letter to her work and to the life that produced it. As a friend and a writer, I am grateful for both.

More than anything, I want to thank Kate for the generosity she has shown – in agreeing to this essay, in being so open with the material, and in how with her own work she has shown me what to do.

Lifeline 13 11 14

BOOKS BY KATE JENNINGS

Mother I'm Rooted (ed.) (1975)
Come to Me My Melancholy Baby (1975)
Women Falling Down in the Street (1990)
Cats, Dogs and Pitchforks (1993)
Bad Manners (1993)
Snake (1996)
Save Me, Joe Louis (1998)
Moral Hazard (2002)
Stanley and Sophie (2008)
Trouble (2010)